FOSSILS, FROGS FISH AND FRIENDS

Principal Writer
Kenneth Ernst, Jr.

Project Director
Richard B. Bliss, Ed.D.

Illustrator
Linda Vance

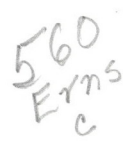

Institute for Creation Research
El Cajon, California

This Supplementary Material was developed as part of a writing project by the Institute for Creation Research.

FOSSILS, FROGS, FISH AND FRIENDS

Published, produced and distributed by the **INSTITUTE for CREATION RESEARCH**

Richard B. Bliss, Ed.D., Project Director

CONSULTANTS

Theodore Fischbacher, Education, Ph.D.
Jean Sloat Morton, Biology, Ph.D.
Gary E. Parker, Biology, Ed.D.
Hazel May Rue, Education, M.S.
Harold S. Slusher, Physics, M.S., D.Sc., Ph.D.

CONTRIBUTING TEAM MEMBERS

ILLUSTRATORS

Shirlene Barrett, Jonathan Chong, Richard Holt, Doug Jennings, Karen Myers, Steve Pitstick, Marvin Ross, Barbara Sauer, Sandy Thornton, Linda Vance, Jay Wegter, Frankie Winn, Tim Lindquist, Ron Fisher, Jeanie Elliott

PROJECT WRITING STAFF

Deborah Bainer—Malaysia
Anne Beams—Germany
Gary G. Eastman—California
Elizabeth Ernst—Oregon
Kenneth F. Ernst, Jr.—Oregon
Olive Fischbacher—California
Norman Fox—Oregon
Virginia Gray Hastings—Illinois
Marilyn F. Hallman—Texas
Alberta Hanson—California
Deborah Hayes—Texas

Richard Holt—Iowa
Melody J. McIntyre—Pennsylvania
Fred Pauling—Virginia
Hazel May Rue—Oregon
Barbara Sauer—Illinois
Wilburn Sooter—Washington
Ivan Stonehocker—Canada
Harold C. Watkins—California
Susan E. Watkins—California
Fred Willson—California

FOSSILS, FROGS, FISH AND FRIENDS

Copyright© 1984
Institute for Creation Research
El Cajon, California 92021

Library of Congress Catalog Card Number 82-71243

ISBN 0-932766-15-3

ALL RIGHTS RESERVED

No part of this publication may be reproduced, stored in a retrieval system, or transmitted by any means—electronic, mechanical, photocopy, recording, or otherwise—without the express prior permission of the Institute for Creation Research, with the exception of brief excerpts in magazine articles and/or reviews.

Cataloging in Publication Data

Ernst, Kenneth
 Fossils, frogs, fish and friends /
author, Kenneth Ernst, Jr. / illustraton,
Linda Vance
 Presents both models of Creation and Evolution.
 1.Fossils—Juvenile literature.
 I. Title II. Vance, Linda
     560

CONTENTS

INTRODUCTION 1
TWO MODELS 3
   Frogs, Fish and Friends
    In The Fossil Record 4
   Chris Offers Some Answers 5
   Evvy Offers Some Answers 7
**ANIMALS WITHOUT
BACKBONES** 10
**HOLD IT! TIME FOR A
FEW QUESTIONS** 15
**FISH, FROGS AND OTHER ANIMALS
WITH BACKBONES** 16
   Origin of Fish 17
HOLD IT! TIME FOR A QUESTION ... 20
THE LAND-WATER ANIMALS 21
CAN WE DECIDE 23
GLOSSARY OF SPECIAL WORDS ... 24
REFERENCES 27
RESOURCE BOOKS 28

PRONUNCIATION KEY

The following pronunciation key is based on the Thorndike-Barnhart School Dictionary. These markings are used in your margin glossary to help you pronounce important words.

hat, āge, fär
let, ēqual, tėrm
it, īce
hot, ōpen, ôrder, oil, out
cup, put, rüle
ch, child
ng, long
sh, she
th, thin
ᵺh, then
zh, measure
uh represents *a* in about, *e* in taken, *i* in pencil,
   o in lemon, *u* in circus

INTRODUCTION

Almost everyone is curious about **fossils*** , especially three friends you'll want to meet.

They are

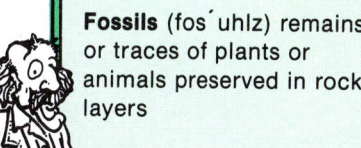

Fossils (fos´uhlz) remains or traces of plants or animals preserved in rock layers

EVVY SMITH,

CHRIS JONES,

and *SURE-ROCK HOLMES*.

Rock hounds (rok houndz) people who hunt fossils and unusual rocks for fun

Data (dā´tuh) a collection of information

They all share the same hobby. They are "**rock hounds**." All three like to dig for fossils and read about fossils found by others. They all have the same **data**, but they have different ideas about what fossils mean.

Evolution (ev uh lü shuhn) a suggested process of simple things changing slowly into complicated things over long periods of time

Evolved (ē välvd´) simple things having changed slowly into complicated things over long periods of time

Creation (krē ā´shuhn) a suggested process by which a Creator made the universe and all life

Evvy believes in **evolution**. She says, "studying fossils lets us see a record of how life evolved."

Chris believes in **creation**. She says, "Fossils show millions of created plants and animals that died in a flood." Chris also believes that the historical account of creation in the Bible is accurate.

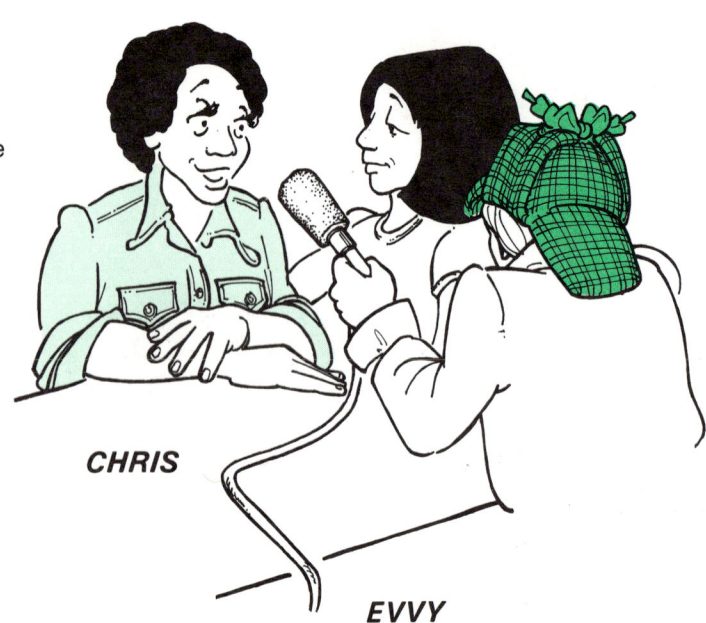

CHRIS

EVVY

Amphibian (am fib´ē uhn) cold-blooded creature such as a frog or a salamander

Fossil record (fos´uhl rek´uhrd) the total collection of all fossils and what we can learn from them

Sure-Rock Holmes hasn't decided what to think. Maybe he's just like you. He tries to be open-minded. He wonders about how and when fossils were made. Or what about the rock layers that contain fossils? Did they form slowly over long ages of time? Did a creator design and make all kinds of life on earth? Did certain fish gradually change into **amphibians**? Does the **fossil record** support evolution or creation? These questions can't be answered completely. But Sure-Rock and other good students can look at the facts in this and other books. Then they can decide what seems to be true.

TWO MODELS

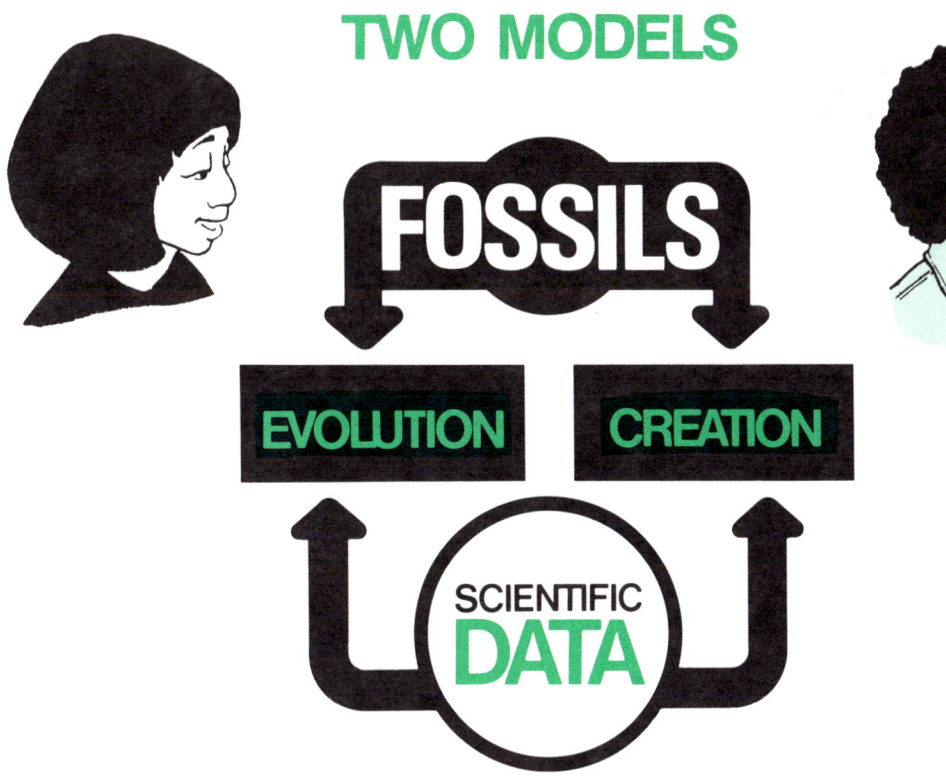

A **"two-model"** study can show us both Evvy's idea (evolution) and Chris' idea (creation) at once. Maybe Sure-Rock can decide for himself what to think. Always remember that a model is not a fact. A model just gives us an idea that facts might fit into.

Two-model (tü mod´l) looking at a problem in two ways

Research has been made on students like you to see how you learn. They found that students learn better when they study both sides of a problem. They learn to think for themselves. Evvy learns why Chris thinks as she does. Chris learns why Evvy has the ideas she has. Sure-Rock has a chance to see both sides. All three can learn new ideas and add to their thinking. This module (short book) will give you the same exciting chances to learn.

FROGS, FISH, AND FRIENDS IN THE FOSSIL RECORD

Just the other day Sure-Rock read that the study of fossils was getting started in the 1800's. During that time a scientist named Darwin came up with the idea of evolution. Many scientists began to replace the old idea of creation with this new idea of Darwin's. They thought the fossil record would help to decide which idea was better.

What would we expect to find in the fossil record if creation were true? What would we expect to find in the fossil record if evolution were true? Let us now try to supply answers to these two important questions.

CHRIS OFFERS SOME ANSWERS

Chris says **creationists** believe that once there were no plants or animals on the earth. All the different, basic kinds of plants and animals were created by a Creator. They were created full grown. Each basic kind would appear in the fossil record complete. (Some kinds, though, would not appear because they are **extinct**.) No **ancestors**, of each kind would be found in an incomplete form. The fossil record should show us, then, that living things came into being suddenly. They came into being in many different, complicated forms. According to this idea, we would expect to find fossils of various basic types similar to those we have today. We would expect to find fossils of fishes and fossils of amphibians. We would not expect to find fossils showing fishes gradually changing into amphibians. For example, sharks would always be sharks. Catfish would always be catfish.

Creationists (krē ā´shuhn uhst) people who believe in creation

Ancestors (an ses tuhrz) members of earlier generations

Extinct (ek stingkt´) not existing now, having died out

We find many invertebrate fossils in the fossil record. These are things such as worms, snails, corals, and starfish.

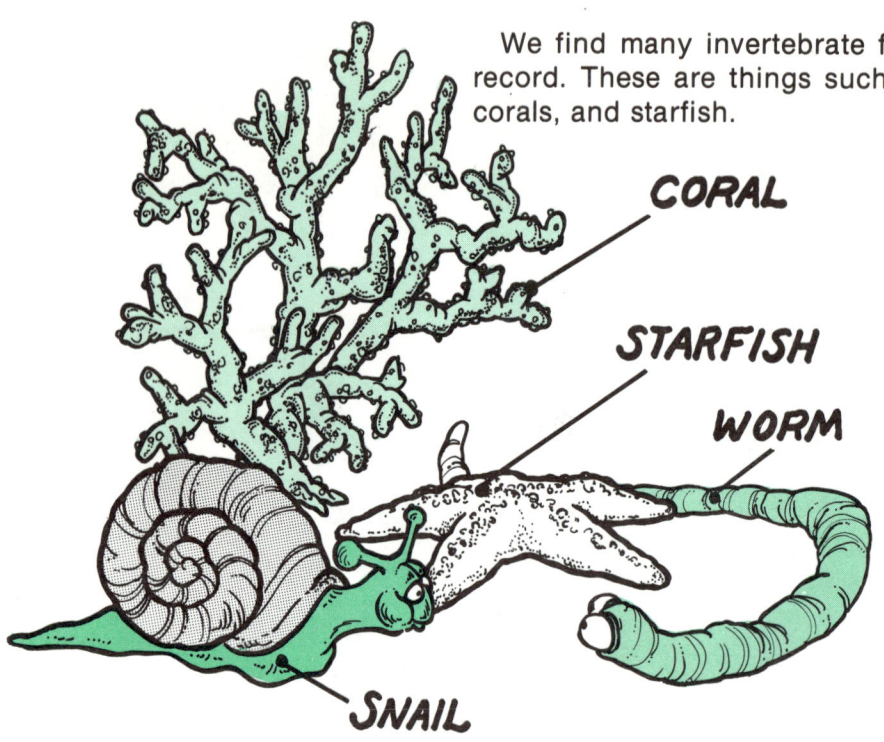

Invertebrates
(in vér´ tuh brits) animals without hard backbones such as worms

No fossils of in-between kinds would appear. We wouldn't find fossils showing **invertebrates** changing slowly into fish. In fact, there should be no in-between types of plants or animals in the fossil record. Figure (1) shows that different kinds of animals can change greatly within the limits of each kind. However, one kind of animal becoming another kind is never seen. Chris said that it isn't surprising to note how well this fits into the Biblical account of creation.

Figure (1)

EVVY OFFERS SOME ANSWERS

Evvy says that **Evolutionists** believe that all living things have evolved from one or a few single-celled beginnings. Evolutionists say that this took many millions of years to happen. Thus, the rocks lowest in the column should have only fossils of very simple life forms.

Evolutionists
(ev uh lü´shuhn uhsts) people who believe in evolution

Fossils higher in the column should be different. They should show a gradual change from these simple forms into more complicated forms of life.

7

Figure (2)

Transitional forms (tran zish´uhn uhl fôrmz) plants and animals with structures and parts that seem to be turning into something else

Therefore, the fossil record should produce many "in-between" types of life. These types are called **transitional forms**. Figure (2) shows in a simple way what an "in-between" thing is like.

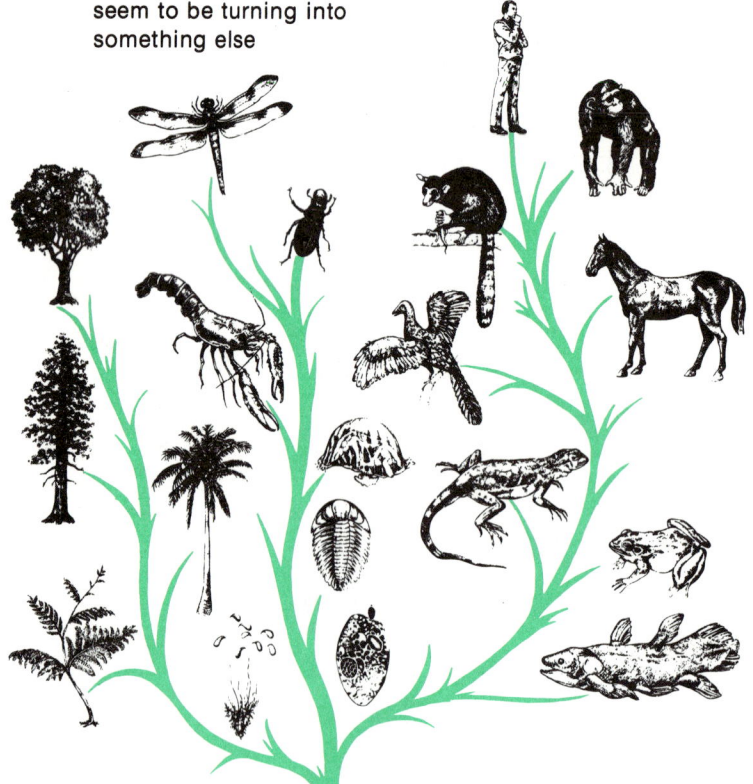

Figure (3)

One would predict, then, that the fossil record would show us something very important. We could trace such things as jellyfish, starfish, and other invertebrates back to their common ancestors.

8

Scientists should be able to find many types "in-between" these creatures. All of life from the present to the past should be closely connected. We should see this in the fossil record. We might show this in a simple way by a drawing. Figure (3) shows how life would have developed from simple forms to more complicated forms.

We can see now what both models predict. Let's look at some fossil evidence, just enough, hopefully to whet your appetite for more. Can you answer the question: "Which model do the facts fit best?" Let's join Evvy, Chris, and Sure-Rock as they investigate the fossil record.

ANIMALS WITHOUT BACKBONES

Sure-Rock has found most animal fossils are shells, casts, molds, and other remains of invertebrates. The animals without backbones include the following: worms, snails, sea urchins, corals, sponges. In some places there are whole hillsides covered with such fossils. Sure-Rock enjoys digging in such hills with his trusty shovel.

The bottoms of some creeks seem to be paved with them. Millions of these fossils from thousands of tons of rock have been collected from around the world. What does this evidence appear to tell us? How were so many animals buried in these places? What could have happened?

Have you seen the kinds of creatures that live in the oceans today? Sure-Rock has! He thinks that Figure (4) is a picture of life off the coast of some South Sea Island. But he's wrong! Figure (4) is a

Figure (4)

model of a display in the American Museum of Natural History. It shows what sea life looked like when these **Cambrian** fossils were alive!

The Cambrian is near the bottom of the **geologic column**, Figure (5). According to the evolution **model**, says Evvy, Cambrian creatures were the first forms of life on earth to leave many fossil remains.

Figure (5)

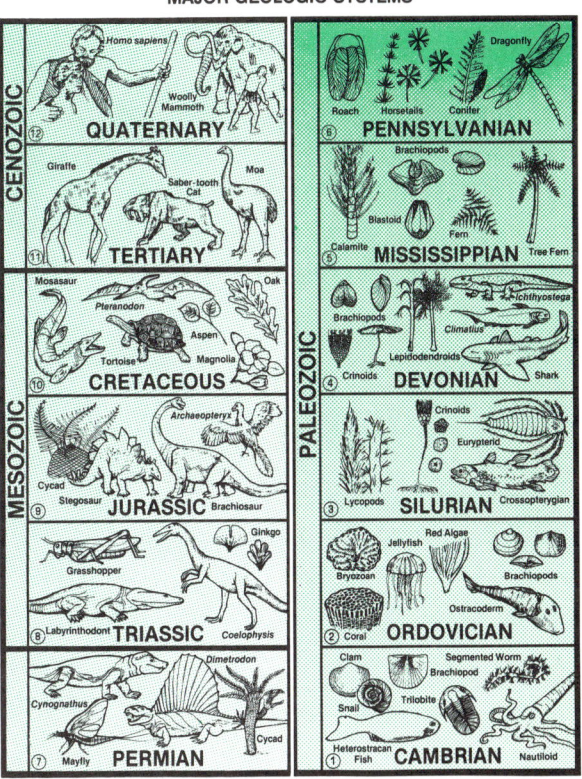

Geologic column (jē´uh loj´ik kol´uhm) a suggested vertical arrangement of rock layers determined in part by the fossils they contain

Model (mod´l) a temporary idea used to interpret facts. Models change with new information.

11

Intermediate
(in´tuhr med´ē uht) located between two things, points, or stages of development

What do we really find in Cambrian rock according to known scientific facts? Can we see any kinds of fossils that would be **intermediate** between clams and snails? Chris says, that according to the creation model, there wouldn't be any. Evvy feels that they'll turn up some day. What do YOU think?

 **Nautiloid** (nă´tuh loid) squid-like animals with straight or coiled shells similar to living pearly Nautilus

(Naughty Lloyd, the 9 foot Nautiloid!)

 **Cuttlefish** (kuht´uhl fish) several types of creatures having arms with suckers and squirting inklike fluid when in danger

Sure-Rock has discovered some more interesting facts. Certain forms of **Cuttlefish** are found right from the "beginning" in Cambrian rock. These Cambrian forms are called **Nautiloids**. They have a long, straight shell. These shells sometimes reach up to 9 feet in length! The modern pearly Nautilus, however, has a coiled shell and many squids do not have a shell.

12

Some fossil corals have a shell and modern ones do not. Fossil snails have minor differences in their twists and **spines**. This allows them to be classified as different **species** of snails. All these creatures are easily seen as snails. They appear much like the modern snails that eat your plants and leave trails on your walks!

Spines (spīnz) the dividing line on the shell

Species (spē´shēz) a group of organisms similar enough to naturally mate together and produce offspring

Sure-Rock has a question for you now. (He thinks he's getting pretty smart because of all the reading he's done!) True or false - "Fossils show that a greater variety of sea life existed in the past than we have today."

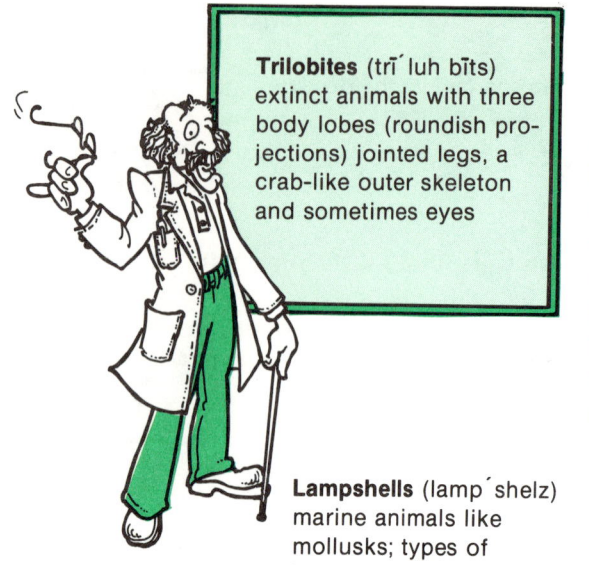

Trilobites (trī´luh bīts) extinct animals with three body lobes (roundish projections) jointed legs, a crab-like outer skeleton and sometimes eyes

Lampshells (lamp´shelz) marine animals like mollusks; types of brachiopods

If you answered "True," then you'd be right. For example, all of the **trilobites** have become extinct. Most of the **lampshells** have become extinct. A few sea lilies survive in the deep ocean, but many that once formed vast undersea gardens are gone forever. Have you ever seen a giant squid? Sure-Rock has, but only as an illustration in a book. Most of the large squid-like animals have become extinct. Only the pearly Nautilus and a few species of shell-less squids and octopi remain.

As you can imagine, Sure-Rock was quite upset about the dying out of so many animals. "What happened"? he asked. "Where did all the nautiloids go?. . .the lampshells?

What do YOU think?

HOLD IT! TIME FOR A FEW QUESTIONS

1. Chris believes that many different living things have existed since creation as clearly different kinds. We now know some facts about Cambrian fossils. Does our new knowledge support Chris' belief?

2. Evvy would say that evolution describes life developing from simple to more complicated and different forms of life. Are Cambrian trilobites simple animals? Do Cambrian snails and clams seem simpler than modern snails and clams?

3. As Sure-Rock has discovered, there are lots of different kinds of invertebrate sea animals in the fossil record. There are many more of these fossil kinds than modern, living kinds. You can see that many have become extinct. Does this favor evolution or creation? Why?

4. Sure-Rock wants to compare the invertebrate fossil facts with the predictions of the evolution and creation models. See if you can help him. Which model seems to fit most facts the best? Give examples of the strongest evidence to support your view.

Vertebrates (vér´ tuh brits) animals with hard backbones, such as birds and mammals

FISH, FROGS, AND OTHER ANIMALS WITH BACKBONES

We have seen that it has not been possible to find in-between forms among major groups of invertebrate fossils. It's a different story for the **vertebrates**, though. Evvy can show us some interesting fossils that she thinks are in-between forms. They would link one group of creatures to another. According to Evvy, these fossils show that some fish gradually changed into amphibians, some amphibians into **reptiles**, and some reptiles into birds, and other reptiles into **mammals** (including man). This is shown in Figure (6).

Reptiles (rep´ tuhls) any cold-blooded vertebrates including turtles, lizards, snakes, crocodilians, and tuatara

Mammals (mam´ uhls) animals with hair or fur whose young are nursed on milk, such as cats and dogs

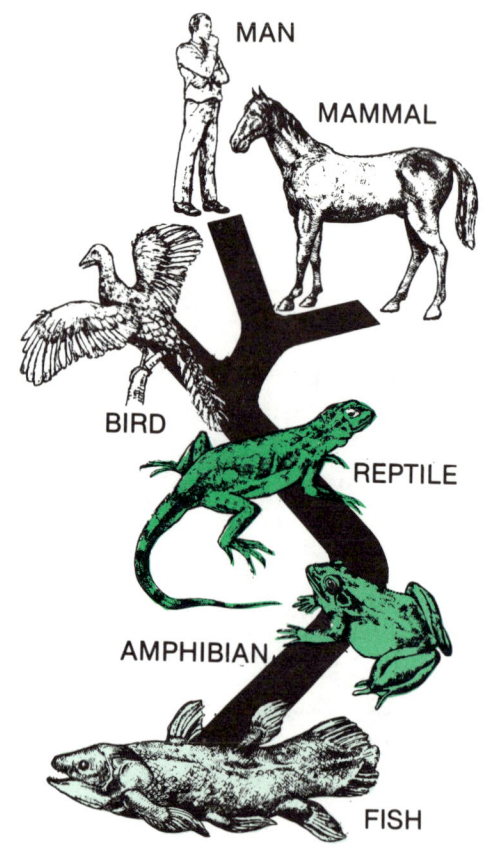

Figure (6)

16

ORIGIN OF FISH

Fish have backbones, Those of you who have caught and cleaned some kind of fish should know this.

Fossil fish are just as bony. Many would have been just as hard to clean.

Evvy says, "There are some fossils that might show how one vertebrate group may have evolved into another."

Sure-Rock discovered, however, that no fossils have ever been found to show how the first vertebrates, the fishes, may have evolved from invertebrate ancestors. Chris isn't surprised by this. Can you figure out why?

Placoderms
(plak´uh dérmz) extinct fish with bony plates (like armor)

Many scientists have studied fish. Sure-Rock read a book by a very respected scientist.[1] He says that no one has been able to find a common ancestor of the bony fishes. He also says extinct fishes like the **placoderms** don't seem to come from anywhere or to go anywhere in the fossil record. Another scientist puts it a different way. He says that there isn't any information about the origins of fish groups.[2]

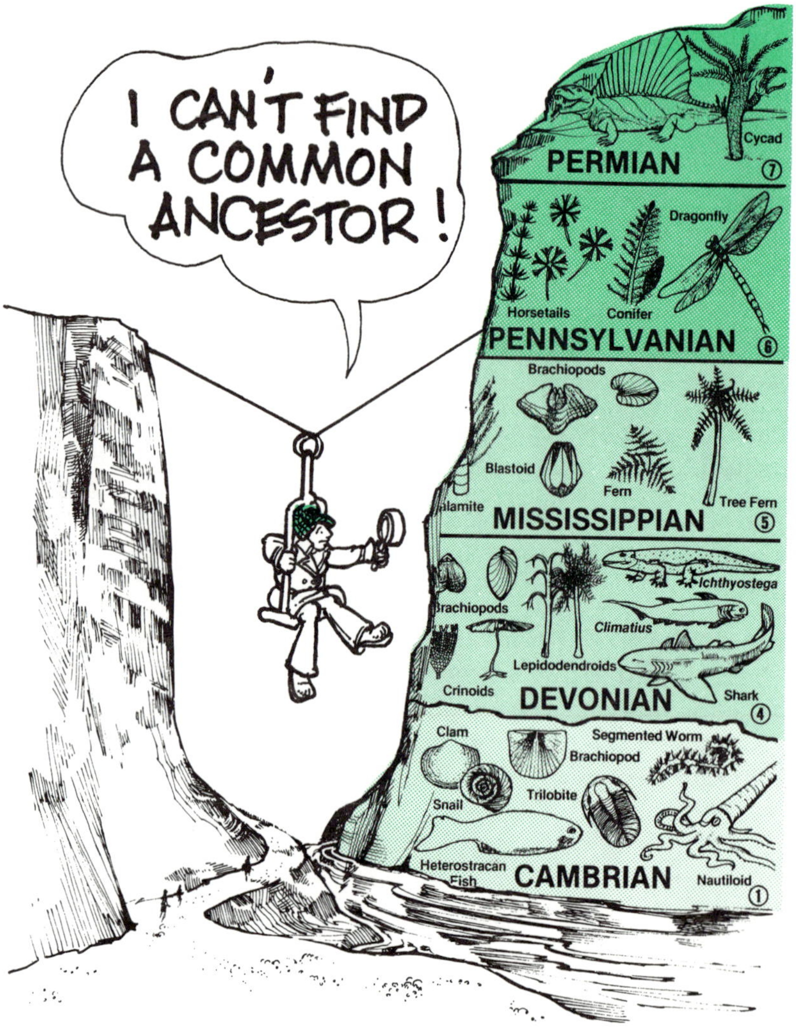

Fish are fairly common in **Devonian** rock. They were once thought to be absent from Cambrian rock. Evvy says, "Many scientists suggest that fish evolved from the invertebrates during these Cambrian times."

Sure-Rock has discovered, however, that there is no evidence of this in the fossil record. He learned this, of course, from reading books about fishes. (You know by now of his habit of reading.)

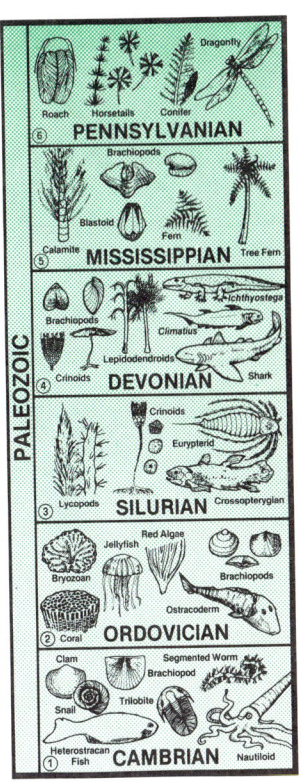

One man even wrote that there is no direct proof or evidence that any of the suggested events or changes ever took place.[3]

Devonian (di vō´nē uhn) a rock layer low in the geologic column containing many fossil fish

Fossils of fish have now been found in upper Cambrian rock. The search for their ancestors must take place in lower Cambrian or Precambrian rocks. Chris says, however, that Precambrian rocks have very, very few, if any, fossils. These rocks seem to offer little hope for success. What do YOU think?

HOLD IT! TIME FOR A QUESTION

1. We now know some things about fossil fish. What conclusions would Chris draw from our new knowledge?...Evvy?

THE LAND-WATER ANIMALS

Have you ever hidden a frog in your teacher's desk? Would she open her drawer and scream, "EEEEK! AMPHIBIAN!"

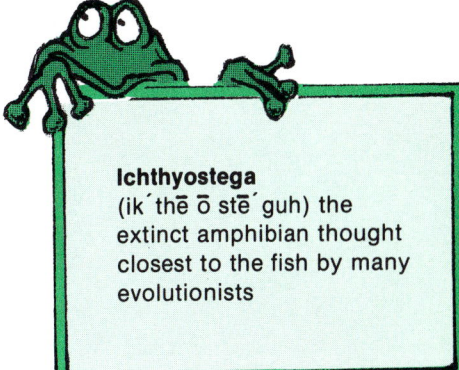

Ichthyostega (ik´ thē ō stē´ guh) the extinct amphibian thought closest to the fish by many evolutionists

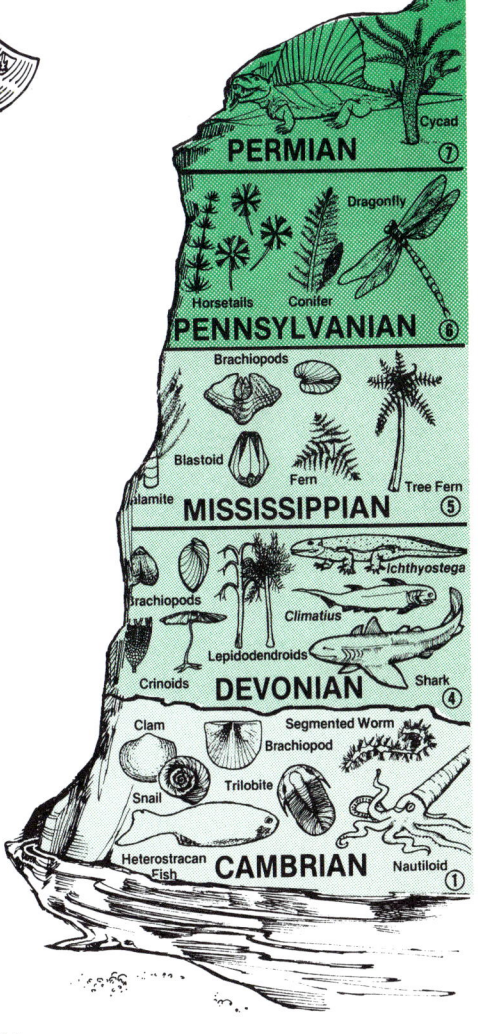

Of course she wouldn't. The point is, however, that slimy-skinned creatures such as frogs and salamanders are called amphibians. They are animals that lead "double lives." First, they are swimming, gill-breathing tadpoles. Then, they live as four-legged, lung breathing adults.

Evvy says, "Two groups of fossils are studied to try to figure out the problem of where amphibians came from. The first group is lobe-finned fishes. The second group is that of the first or lowest amphibian in the geologic column **Ichthyostega**."

Figure (7) shows the lobe-finned fish and the amphibian, Ichthyostega. The bone pattern in its fin is somewhat similar to the pattern in your arm. It is also similar to the leg of a frog.

21

Figure (7)

Lobe-finned fish are still alive today. They include forms that can use their swim bladders somewhat like lungs. These fish also had complicated vertebrae (backbones) like those found in the first amphibian. Teeth and some parts of the skull are similar. Some are not. Based on these likenesses, Evvy would suppose that amphibians evolved from these fishes.

Chris would say that lobe-finned fish do not show evolution from a common ancestor. Rather, they show creation according to a common plan. She would also say that these fish are in some ways similar to Ichthyostega. However, they are similar only because they had a common Designer.

Here is a tough problem. We've given you and Sure-Rock a lot of facts to digest.

If you're confused about anything, you might want to read the information again. Evvy says the similarities between these creatures support evolution. Chris says the differences support creation. What do YOU think?

CAN WE DECIDE?

Sure-Rock Holmes has come to one conclusion. It seems to him that both Chris and Evvy have unsolved problems.

Chris believes that the fossil record shows that many created kinds of animals died in a flood. She also points out that this flood is consistent with the historical, Biblical account of a flood. She says there is no reason to believe that this Flood catastrophe did not cover all of the earth. Evvy believes the fossil record shows how some kinds of animals evolved into other kinds. But Sure-Rock wonders why there aren't lots of in-between forms of life among these kinds.

Studying fossils is like exploring a mystery without all the evidence. What if two fossils are alike in some ways? Evvy may think they are similar because one evolved from the other. Chris would say it is because the same Designer made both. The fossils alone can't tell us. The facts could be explained in more than one way. In any case, it is scientifically wrong to make the facts fit a model that can't work.

You've looked at many facts in the light of two opposite ideas. We hope you were stirred to think for yourself. Finally, we hope you will be courteous toward other people's ideas.

GLOSSARY OF SPECIAL WORDS

Amphibian: cold-blooded creature such as a frog or a salamander

Ancestors: members of earlier generations

Cambrian: thought to be the oldest stratum (rock layer) where fossil life forms can be found

Creation: a suggested process by which a Creator made the universe and all life

Creationists: people who believe in creation

Cuttlefish: several types of creatures having arms with suckers and squirting inklike fluid when in danger

Data: a collection of information

Devonian: a rock layer low in the geologic column containing many fossil fish

Evolution: a suggested process of simple things changing slowly into complicated things over long periods of time

Evolutionists: people who believe in evolution

Evolved: simple things having changed slowly into complicated things over long periods of time

Extinct: not existing now, having died out

Fossils: remains or traces of plants or animals preserved in rock layers

Fossil record: the total collection of all fossils and what we can learn from them

Geologic column: a suggested vertical arrangement of rock layers determined in part by the fossils they contain

Ichthyostega: the extinct amphibian thought closest to the fish by many evolutionists

GLOSSARY

Intermediate: located between two things, points, or stages of development

Invertebrates: animals without hard backbones such as worms

Lampshells: marine animals like mollusks; types of brachiopods

Mammals: animals with hair or fur whose young are nursed on milk, such as cats and dogs

Model: a temporary idea used to interpret facts. Models change with new information

Nautiloids: squid-like animals with straight or coiled shells similar to living pearly Nautilus

Placoderms: extinct fish with bony plates (like armor)

Reptiles: any cold-blooded vertebrates including turtles, lizards, snakes, crocodilians, and tuatara

Rock hounds: people who hunt fossils and unusual rocks for fun

Species: a group or organisms similar enough to naturally mate together and produce offspring

Spines: the dividing line on the shell

Transitional forms: plants and animals with structures and parts that seem to be turning into something else

Trilobites: extinct animals with three body lobes (roundish projections) jointed legs, a crab-like outer skeleton and sometimes eyes

Two-model: looking at a problem in two ways

Vertebrates: animals with hard backbones, such as birds and mammals

REFERENCES

1. **Romer, A.S.,** *Vertebrate Paleontology,* Chicago: University of Chicago Press, 1966, pp. 15-16.

2. **White, Errol,** *Proceedings of the Linnean Society of London,* Vol. 177, 1966, p. 8.

3. **Ommany, F.D.,** *The Fishes,* Time-Life, Life Nature Library, 1964, p. 60.

RESOURCE BOOKS

EVOLUTION:

Gastonguay, Paul R., *Evolution for Everyone,* (Biological Science Curriculum Study), Bobbs Merrill Co., Inc., Indianapolis, 1974.

Rhodes, F.H.T., et. at., *Fossils: A Guide to Prehistoric Life,* Godden Press, NY, 1972.

Wood, Peter, et al., *Life Before Man,* Time-Life Books, NY, 1972.

CREATION:

Gish, Duane T., *Evolution: The Fossils Say No!,* Creation-Life Publishers, San Diego, 1973.

Moore, John N. and **Harold S. Slusher,** Eds., *Biology: A Search for Order in Complexity,* Zondervan, Grand Rapids, MI, 1970.

Morris, Henry M., *Scientific Creationism,* Creation-Life Publishers, San Diego, 1974.

Parker, Gary, et al., *Fossils: Key to the Present,* Creation-Life Publishers, San Diego, 1979.

TWO-MODEL:

Bliss, Richard B., *Origins: Two Models,* Creation-Life Publishers, San Diego, 1978.